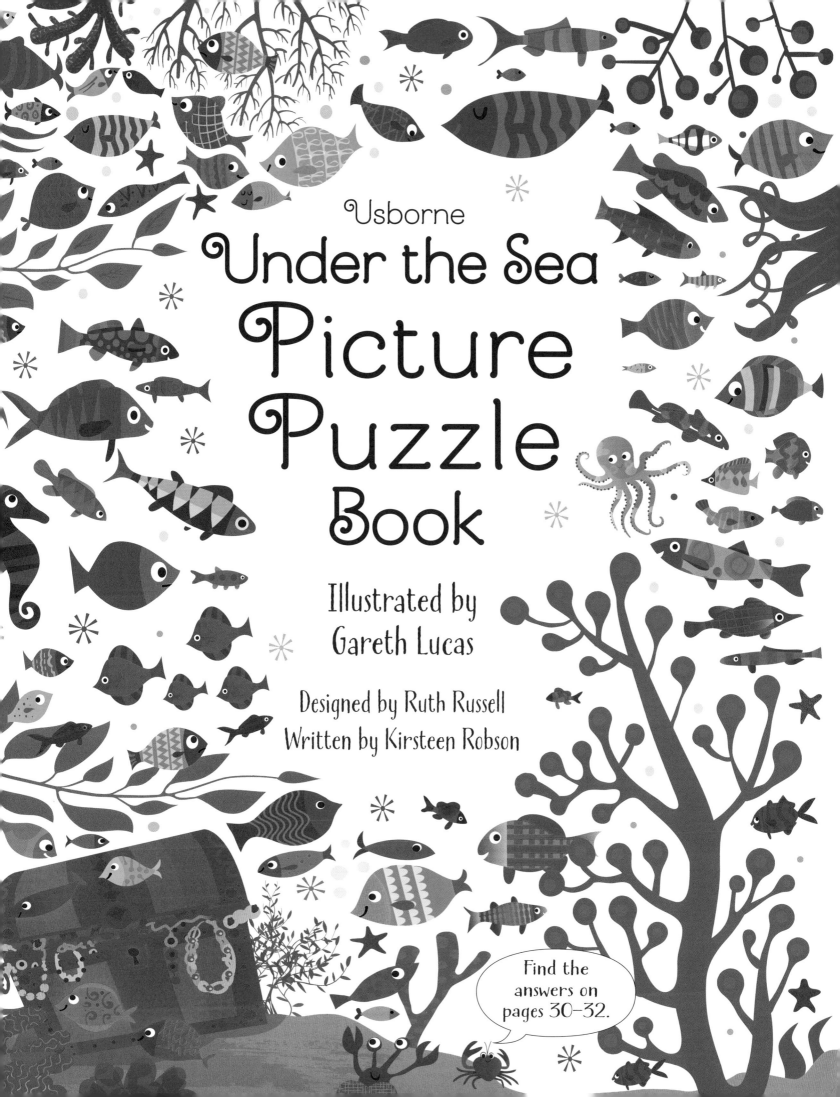

Usborne
Under the Sea
Picture
Puzzle
Book

Illustrated by
Gareth Lucas

Designed by Ruth Russell
Written by Kirsteen Robson

Find the
answers on
pages 30–32.

15

20

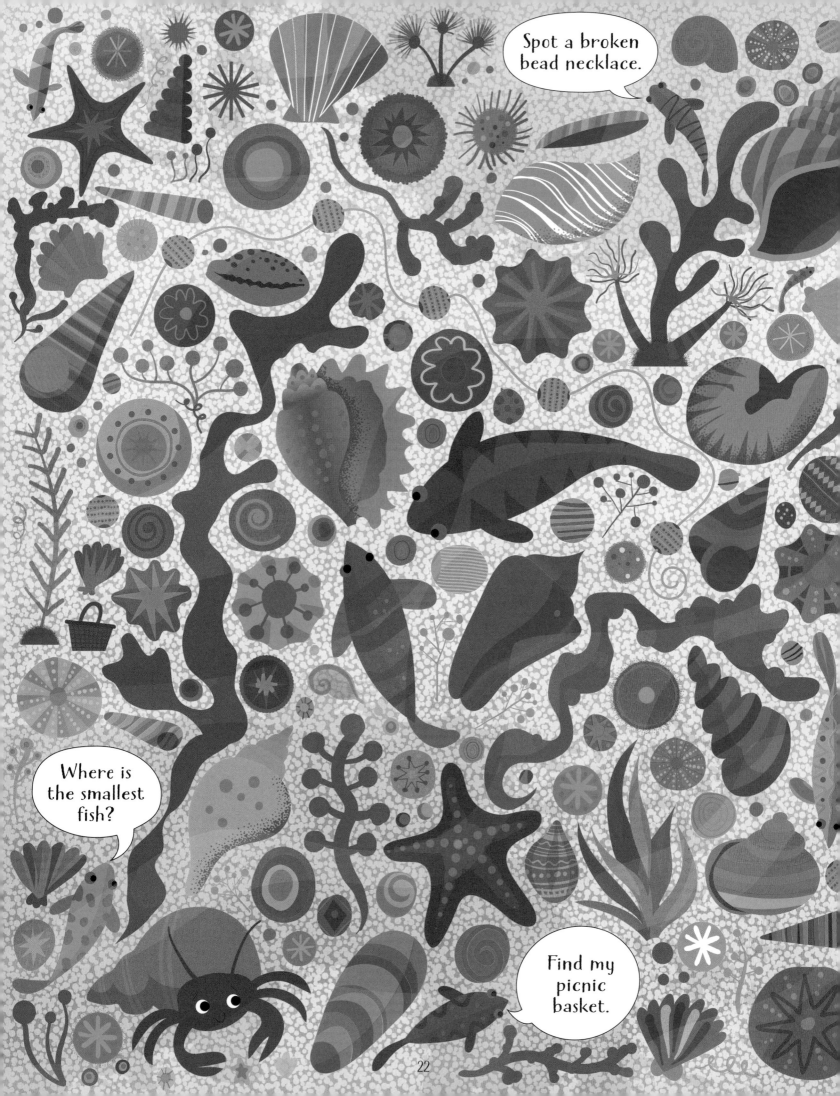

ANSWERS

Cover

1

2-3

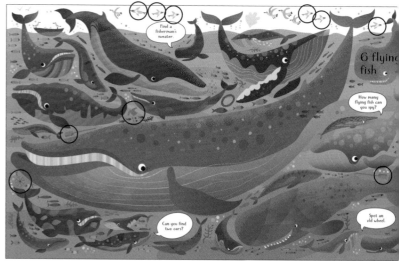

4-5

6-7

8-9

10–11

12–13

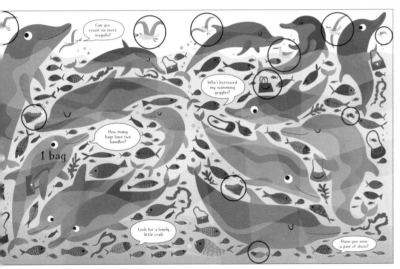

14–15

16–17

18–19

20–21

ANSWERS (continued)

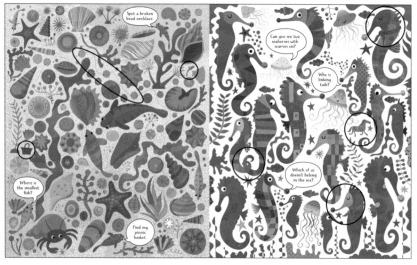

22-23

24-25

26-27

28-29